BEYOND A **SALES PERSON** IS A

INCREASING **PERFORMANCE** I

INDUSTR

# The Sales Professionals

# WORKBOOK

**By Nathan Jamail**

TO BE USED IN CONJUNCTION WITH ***THE SALES PROFESSIONALS PLAYBOOK***

Improve confidence!

Increase sales and profits!

Improve skills and abilities!

Become a professional!

# Workbook Description

This workbook works in conjunction with *The Sales Professionals Playbook*. Reading the playbook and completing the exercises in this workbook will help you develop the skills you need to become a successful sales professional. These exercises are not based on theory, but rather on proven techniques and practices that have allowed hundreds of sales professionals to find success!

This workbook is intended for small workgroups or individual use. Sales professionals will learn skills and proven models that will:

- Improve confidence
- Improve skills and abilities
- Improve professionalism
- Increase sales and profits

What you will need to complete this workbook:

- A copy of *The Sales Professionals Playbook*
- Pen or pencil
- Printed copy of this workbook
- An open and ready mind

*Let's get started!*

**Professional Salesmanship** **Chapter 1**

Pro·fess·ion·al [pruh-fesh-uh-nl] adj. 1. *Participating for gain or livelihood in an activity or field.*

Welcome to the field. The game is professional salesmanship, and you're working on the playbook for professional sales. Anyone with a voice and a smile can be a salesperson, but it takes a skilled, driven, and eager-to-learn person to be a successful sales professional. This section presents and overview of what professional salesmanship requires.

*What is the difference between a sales person and a sales professional?*

_______________________________________________

_______________________________________________

*Avoid stupid stuff people say (things that may ring true, but are too generic to yield real value). Fill in the blank with stupid descriptions people sometimes say about sales:*

Sales is a __________________ game

Sales is a _____________________ business

Other(s) that you may have heard:

_______________________________________________

_______________________________________________

**Circle the following descriptions that are true of sales professionals:**

- Not a noble career
- Requires achievement of one of the most difficult skills
- Takes passion and confidence
- No practice necessary
- Are *proud* of what they do for a living.

**Current Activities**: Please circle "Yes" if you are currently doing the following on a regular basis and "No" if you are not:

| | | |
|---|---|---|
| Regular skills practice | Yes | No |
| Scrimmaging (role play) on a daily or weekly basis | Yes | No |
| You currently have a written game plan (business/sales plan) | Yes | No |
| You desire to be the best in your organization | Yes | No |

What are some things you can do to take your sales professionalism to a higher level?

______________________________________________________________________

______________________________________________________________________

______________________________________________________________________

______________________________________________________________________

______________________________________________________________________

______________________________________________________________________

**Practicing for Profits**

When was the last time you practiced (really practiced) a skill? ____________________

What did you practice? ______________________________________________

Was it effective? _________ Why or why not? ______________________________

______________________________________________________________________

What skill would you like to practice right now if you could (i.e., what you feel could use the most improvement)?_________________________________________________

Would your customers call you a sales professional or a sales person? _______________

*Above all, remember to practice!*

## Principals of Influential Selling — Chapter 2

sell'ing [sel-ing] v. 1. *To exchange or deliver for money.*

When I think of "old school" selling techniques, I'm often reminded of the cheesy 1980 movie *Used Cars*. The comedy, which holds a place of honor in my DVD collection, stars Kurt Russell as a hotshot used car salesman named Rudy Russo. Russo and his crew are getting piece-of-junk cars ready to sell, and they willing try anything to make a sale. This is indicative of what many customers view as the sales process. It is a sales professionals job to change that outlook using the principles of influential selling.

**Influential selling is based on four key principals:**

- No one likes to be sold, but everybody likes to buy things.
- People generally buy with their emotions and justify with logic.
- Treat prospective customers as if they're your mom.
- Establish likability, trust, and influence.

Describe a situation in which YOU bought something and felt like you were being manipulated in the sale:

____________________________________________________________

____________________________________________________________

Why? What could the sales person have done differently?

____________________________________________________________

____________________________________________________________

In your own words, describe the difference between a sales professional and a sales person:

____________________________________________________________

____________________________________________________________

**Principals of Influential Selling**

*People buy things with emotions and justify with logic.*

*Fill in the blank*: Moods are ___________________.

So, if this is the case, what kind of mood or tone should you set during the sales call?

_______________________________________________________________________

*Treat prospective customers as if they are your mom.*

If your product is truly not a fit for the prospective client, what should you do?

_______________________________________________________________________

Why? _________________________________________________________________

*Establish likability, trust and influence with your prospective customer!*

People do business with people they ________________. Just because they like you _____________ mean they will do business with you. They have to ________ you. If someone likes you and trusts you, you then need to be viewed as an ______________ in order to continue a business relationship. A customer must experience all three virtues of influential selling in order to __________ make a buying decision.

**Reaching the Goal**

Prospective customers must like us, trust us and clearly see our professional knowledge and our sincere concern for their happiness. Only then will they look to us as the sales professional who can give them the best advice. Describe a scenario in which you failed to reach all three virtues of influential selling and did not close the sale. What could you have done differently?

_______________________________________________________________________

_______________________________________________________________________

_______________________________________________________________________

*Above all, remember to practice!*

Lik·a·bl·it·y (lī-kə-'bi-lə-tē) adj. 1. *Easy to like; pleasing*

In old school business-to-business selling, we were taught to find something in our prospect's office to relate to and use to spark a conversation. In theory the lesson was simple and wise. In the field, though, it proves to be ill advised as it comes across as insincere and forced. What does it take then to be a *likable* sales professional?

**Be YOU, be confident**

Throughout the sales process you should always be _____________.

Describe a time you tried to be someone you weren't in order to connect with a customer:

______________________________________________________________

______________________________________________________________

What are some true things about yourself that you can use to connect with someone (hobbies, family, education, sports, etc):

- ______________________________
- ______________________________
- ______________________________
- ______________________________
- ______________________________
- ______________________________
- ______________________________

trust (trŭst) n. 1. *Firm reliance on the integrity, ability, or character of a person or thing*

Now that we have learned to establish likability, it is time to move across the field, put on some new equipment, and earn the trust of our prospective customers. Remember, just because they like us, does not mean they are going to do business with us. We must *earn* their trust.

Instead of asking qualifying and leading questions, ask ____________________ and __________________ questions.

**You have only one thing to sell. That is ___________.**

***Developing Questions***

**To build trust is to focus on three key points:**

1. People buy emotionally and justify logically.
2. Why they should buy from you how you are different.
3. The WIIFM for the prospective customer (what's in it for them).

Why should a potential customer buy from you? (Do not use the standards of "great customer service, you care, or your people make the difference"):

______________________________________________________________________

______________________________________________________________________

______________________________________________________________________

***Developing Questions***

**WIIFM:** *What's In It For Me?*

What is our tangible value to the customer?

Everybody responds to this question with "great customer service, integrity, a proven track record, etc." What else? *What can we prove?*

1.

2.

3.

4.

**WIIFM statement:** This statement tells a person who you are, what you do, and why they should know you (your WIIFM), and it should take only 25 seconds or less to say.

*Example:* My name is Nathan; I am with Dry Clean Super Center. We are a family-owned and operated full service dry cleaners. We have discount prices with a full price, full service approach. Most importantly, our employees know that treating customers with exceptional appreciation is just as important as cleaning the clothes.

*What is your WIIFM?*

______________________________________________________________________

______________________________________________________________________

______________________________________________________________________

______________________________________________________________________

______________________________________________________________________

______________________________________________________________________

______________________________________________________________________

______________________________________________________________________

***Developing Questions***

Name five aspects of your industry as a whole that clients tend not to like:

*(This information will help develop the* **why** *of the purposeful questions)*

1.
2.
3.
4.
5.

Name three aspects of your industry as a whole that clients tend to believe are important:

1.
2.
3.

Bring up any competitive disadvantages. If you don't, the potential customer will, when you are not there to discuss them. What are some?

______________________________________________

______________________________________________

______________________________________________

______________________________________________

______________________________________________

How would you bring these competitive disadvantages up in the conversation?

______________________________________________

______________________________________________

______________________________________________

______________________________________________

______________________________________________

**Developing Questions**

Just like a storybook, you want to start with "once upon a time" and end with "happily ever after." Order matters! Develop your purposeful questions in the correct order and have an effective and consistent flow. Start wide and go narrow.

As sales professionals we must accept that the service or product we are selling to a prospective customer is most likely just a fraction of the prospects focus and concerns. By understanding their position and perspective we are better positioned to show how our product or service *can* benefit their overall issues or goals.

**Starting wide:** Industry and then Company
**Going narrow:** Person, Current Vendor, and then Product or service

Why do you think it's best to start wide and go narrow?

____________________________________________________________

____________________________________________________________

____________________________________________________________

What would likely happen to a sales call during which the questioning progressed from the narrow to the wide?

____________________________________________________________

____________________________________________________________

____________________________________________________________

*Keep in mind the five things we listed as industry pain points or facts that affect the prospect. What are these?*

1.
2.
3.
4.
5.

**Developing Questions**

*Let's create the questions!*

Example: What is the question and response you are looking for and why?

> **Question**: What is your position in the market place? Are you the cheapest or most expensive?
>
> **Desired Answer**: We are not the most expensive, but we are not the cheapest either; we are a high value provider.
>
> **Why**: Helps me overcome any pricing issues in the future.

Now, let's create questions about the prospect's company, current vendor, product and service.

We'll start with five questions about **industry**.

Example: Tell me about your industry? (e.g., is business good, number of competitors?)

1. Question: ____________________
   Desired Answer: ____________________
   Why: ____________________

2. Question: ____________________
   Desired Answer: ____________________
   Why: ____________________

3. Question: ____________________
   Desired Answer: ____________________
   Why: ____________________

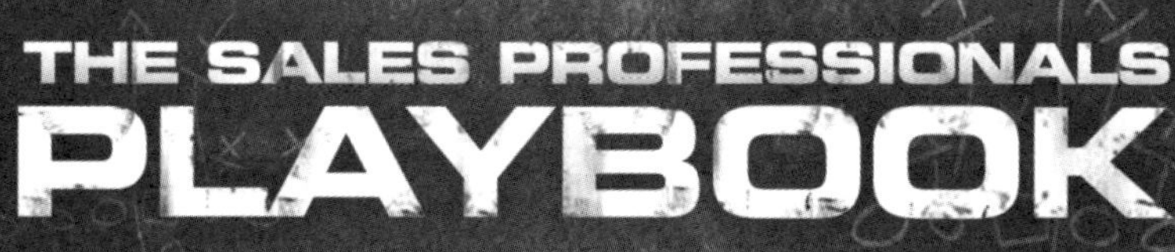




**Industry Continued**

4. Question:______________________________
   Desired Answer: __________________________
   Why: ________________________________

5. Question:______________________________
   Desired Answer: __________________________
   Why: ________________________________

**Company:**

Example: What makes you different than your competitors?

1. Question: ______________________________
   Desired Answer: __________________________
   Why: ________________________________

2. Question: ______________________________
   Desired Answer: __________________________
   Why: ________________________________

3. Question: ______________________________
   Desired Answer: __________________________
   Why: ________________________________

4. Question: ______________________________
   Desired Answer: __________________________
   Why: ________________________________

5. Question: ______________________________
   Desired Answer: __________________________
   Why: ________________________________

**Person:**

Example: What are your top three priorities this year?

1. Question: ______________________________
   Desired Answer: ______________________________
   Why: ______________________________

2. Question: ______________________________
   Desired Answer: ______________________________
   Why: ______________________________

3. Question: ______________________________
   Desired Answer: ______________________________
   Why: ______________________________

4. Question: ______________________________
   Desired Answer: ______________________________
   Why: ______________________________

**Competitor:**

Example: If you had a magic wand and could change anything about your current service, what would it be?

1. Question: ______________________________
   Desired Answer: ______________________________
   Why: ______________________________

2. Question: ______________________________
   Desired Answer: ______________________________
   Why: ______________________________

**Competitor Continued**

3. Question: ______________________________
   Desired Answer: ______________________________
   Why: ______________________________

4. Question: ______________________________
   Desired Answer: ______________________________
   Why: ______________________________

**Product or Service:**

Example: Have your needs or use of the product or service changed in the past 12 months, and if so how?

1. Question: ______________________________
   Desired Answer: ______________________________
   Why: ______________________________

2. Question: ______________________________
   Desired Answer: ______________________________
   Why: ______________________________

3. Question: ______________________________
   Desired Answer: ______________________________
   Why: ______________________________

4. Question: ______________________________
   Desired Answer: ______________________________
   Why: ______________________________

*Above all, remember to practice!*

so·lu·tion (sə-lōō′ shən) n. 1. *The method or process of solving a problem*

Your prospective customers like you, they trust you, and now it's time they are influenced by you. If you are thinking that this stage presents the most difficult challenge so far, you are correct. Not only do you have to succeed at what it takes to influence your customers, you have to remain a likeable and trustworthy sales professional all the while.

What does it mean to *you* to be an influencer?

______________________________________________

______________________________________________

**Keeping the Trust**

Transitioning from asking purposeful questions to proposing a solution can mean treading dangerous ground. Why?

______________________________________________

______________________________________________

*Making the transition requires:*

G _ _ _ _ _

K _ _ _ _ _ _ _ _ _

and, P _ _ _ _ _ _ _ _

**Closing**

If you have established all three positions (likeability, trust and influence), you have a right to _____ for the sale.

What are some reasons you have not asked for the sale?

List different closing statements that you can use:

1:

2:

3:

*Above all, remember to practice!*

plan (pl ā̆n) n. 1. *A scheme, program, or method worked out beforehand for the accomplishment of an objective*

Without a game plan, even the most talented football team will not be prepared for the plays of an opposing team. As sales professionals we tend to think that we don't need to plan; we just need to get out there and do it. This is the 1st step to failing.

A plan gives a sales professional a clear sense of where one is, where to go and what to do, step-by-step, to get there.

A plan in your head is not a plan; it is a T __ __ __ __ __ __.

*Write. It. Down.*

**Goals, expectations and plays**

Do you currently have a sales plan? Yes No Do you use it? Yes No

Your plan should never look N __ __. It should be used, tattered and referenced (a few coffee stains are ok too).

**Three components**

***1: Where are you now and what are you doing now*** (include your current results and your current activities):

Previous Quarter____________________

Previous Year (same time) __________________

**Creating Your Sales Plan**

*Selling Activities (each activity should include a time allocation, for example: Cold call Friday's 10am-11am)*

Current clients:

____________________________________________________________

____________________________________________________________

____________________________________________________________

____________________________________________________________

New clients/prospects:

____________________________________________________________

____________________________________________________________

____________________________________________________________

____________________________________________________________

Prospecting activities:

____________________________________________________________

____________________________________________________________

____________________________________________________________

____________________________________________________________

Upcoming appointments/events:

____________________________________________________________

____________________________________________________________

____________________________________________________________

____________________________________________________________

Other:

____________________________________________________________

____________________________________________________________

____________________________________________________________

***2: Where do you want to go?*** For this component use two sets of goals; long-term annual goals and short-term quarterly goals (annual goals are results based, where quarterly goals are going to be both activity-based and results-based):

*Annual Goals:*
1.______________________
2.______________________
3.______________________
4.______________________
5.______________________

*Quarterly Goals:*
1.______________________
2.______________________
3.______________________
4.______________________
5.______________________

***3: How are you going to get there?*** This is one of the most important parts of your sales plan and where the magic really happens. Think of two things: 1) who you are going to contact and 2) how you are going to contact them.

*Who is your target market?*

______________________________________________

______________________________________________

*How and **when** will you contact your target market?*

______________________________________________

______________________________________________

*Prospect list 1 (vertical market):*
1.______________________
2.______________________
3.______________________
4.______________________
5.______________________

*Prospect list 2 (current customer referrals):*
1.______________________
2.______________________
3.______________________
4.______________________
5.______________________

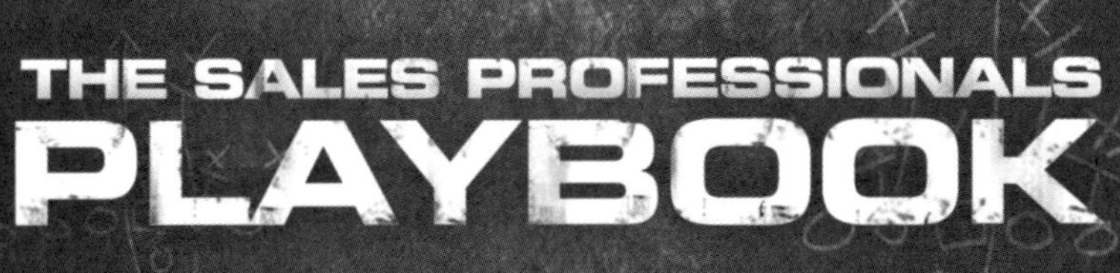




*Company expectations:*

1:________________________________________

2:________________________________________

3:________________________________________

4:________________________________________

5:________________________________________

6:________________________________________

7:________________________________________

8:________________________________________

*Expectations of myself:*

1:________________________________________

2:________________________________________

3:________________________________________

4:________________________________________

5:________________________________________

6:________________________________________

7:________________________________________

8:________________________________________

*Scrimmage plan (list dates/time/where and who you will practice with):*

Date/Time: ____________ With whom: ____________ Where: ____________
What (or focus): ____________________________________

Date/Time: ____________ With whom: ____________ Where: ____________
What (or focus): ____________________________________

Date/Time: ____________ With whom: ____________ Where: ____________
What (or focus): ____________________________________

**Accountability**

Share your plan! By sharing your plan, you have recruited others to help hold you accountable. If your boss does not require a plan; *do it anyhow*. List those that you can share your plan with (those that will help you be accountable to it):

1:_______________________________________
2:_______________________________________
3:_______________________________________

**Review and adjust quarterly**

By sharing your plan, you not only ensure some accountability, you will also gain ideas to adjust your plan. This also allows you to gain new best practices!

List some best practices that you have learned from others over the last six months:

1:_______________________________________. Did you use it? Yes No
Why? _______________________________________

2:_______________________________________. Did you use it? Yes No
Why? _______________________________________

3:_______________________________________. Did you use it? Yes No
Why? _______________________________________

4:_______________________________________. Did you use it? Yes No
Why? _______________________________________

5:_______________________________________. Did you use it? Yes No
Why? _______________________________________

*Above all, remember to practice!*

**Practice Makes Profit** **Chapter 8**

prac•tice ('prak tes) v. 1. *To exercise one's self in, for improvement, or to acquire discipline or dexterity*

Sports teams and athletes spend 90% of their time practicing and 10% of their time playing the game. In sales, however, we spend less than 1% of the time practicing and 99% of our time playing the game. If a successful sales team requires the same elements that make up a successful sports team (like a great leader, drafting the best players, teamwork, positive mental attitudes, etc.), then why are we overlooking the most important element—practice?

Practice is not T __ __ __ __ __ __ __. It is *practicing*.

**Important Note:** One of the things that professional sales people hate the most is role-playing. Let's take that word out of our vocabulary and use "scrimmage" instead. In sports, playing the game is the most fun, while scrimmaging next. Our sales calls are the most fun, so scrimmaging (practicing) should be the next.

**Developing a plan**

A practice schedule is critical: weekly, monthly and quarterly at a minimum. Let's develop your practice plan!

*Topics for practicing* (i.e. selling skills, negotiation skills, closing skills, etc. You should continue to work on each one, then rotate back to the 1st one and start over):
1: ______________________________
2: ______________________________
3: ______________-[______________
4: ______________________________
5: ______________________________
6: ______________________________
7: ______________________________
8: ______________________________
9: ______________________________
10: ______________________________

**The schedule**: *the when, where and how to practice* (take the time to fill in your plan for the next month and the quarter):

*Weekly* (List a time to do a weekly practice—it doesn't have to take longer than 45-60 minutes):

Month 1, week #1

When ____________________ Where ____________________

How ________________________________________

Topic ________________________________________

Month 1, week #2

When ____________________ Where ____________________

How ________________________________________

Topic ________________________________________

Month 1, week #3

When ____________________ Where ____________________

How ________________________________________

Topic ________________________________________

Month 1, week #4

When ____________________ Where ____________________

How ________________________________________

Topic ________________________________________

Month 1, week #5 (if applicable)

When ____________________ Where ____________________

How ________________________________________

Topic ________________________________________

*Monthly* (list a time, place and with whom to do a monthly practice—this can be done in one to three hours):

When ______________________________ Where ________________________________

With whom (peer, another team, etc.) __________________________________________

How ______________________________________________________________________

Topic (s) __________________________________________________________________

*Quarterly* (list a time, place and with whom to do a quarterly practice—this can be three to six hours…include a mock agenda/outline):

When ______________________________ Where ________________________________

With whom (peer, another team, etc.) __________________________________________

How ______________________________________________________________________

Topic (s) __________________________________________________________________

Agenda (start time, flow of time allocated by topic/type of practice, end time and any role or responsibility assignment—you can incorporate a team builder if desired as well):

___________________________________________________________________________

___________________________________________________________________________

___________________________________________________________________________

___________________________________________________________________________

___________________________________________________________________________

___________________________________________________________________________

___________________________________________________________________________

___________________________________________________________________________

___________________________________________________________________________

___________________________________________________________________________

___________________________________________________________________________

*You can plan out an entire year-so don't stop here!*

**Prioritizing practice**

Salesmanship is one of the hardest professions; it is formed of intangibles. Without practice, a professional will become unprofessional, lackluster and behind the competition.

When was the last time you practiced? ________________________________________
What do you remember learning or taking to apply in what you do? _________________

______________________________________________________________________

**Commitment to getting better**

Practicing, or scrimmaging, should be *fun*. Think about your next appointment; the very next one coming up. Now think of a peer or someone you trust that you can scrimmage with. Write this down:

Next appointment is when ______________________ with whom ________________
Who can you scrimmage with ___________________________ when ______________

Call and schedule it…***now***.

*Be coachable*
When was the last time you received feedback on a specific part of your selling skills or performance? ____________________________________________________________
What was the feedback? __________________________________________________
Did you implement it (why or why not) ____________________________________
The idea is to treat practice like you would the biggest appointment you have. You wouldn't reschedule the biggest appointment you have …would you?

*Above all, remember to practice!*

**Building Your Prospect Pipeline** **Chapter 9**

pros·pect (prŏs´ pĕkt´) n. 1. *A potential customer, client, or purchaser*

Prospecting is not waiting for your phone to ring, or emails to come through asking for your business. Prospecting is just what it sounds like; going OUT and finding the business.

**Knowing whom to contact**

A true professional sales person has a plan (remember the plan?) to identify prospects to call and developing a solid prospect sphere. **Important:** why is it necessary to have permission to contact?

______________________________________________________________________

A prospect sphere is divided into two lists: monthly and quarterly. To start, who is likely to give you new business, now? Let's write down some names:

1: ____________________________________
2: ____________________________________
3: ____________________________________
4: ____________________________________
5: ____________________________________

Next let's identify our monthly and quarter lists (this is a starting point):

*Monthly*

1: ____________________________
2: ____________________________
3: ____________________________
4: ____________________________
5: ____________________________
6: ____________________________
7: ____________________________
8: ____________________________
9: ____________________________
10: ____________________________
11: ____________________________
12: ____________________________

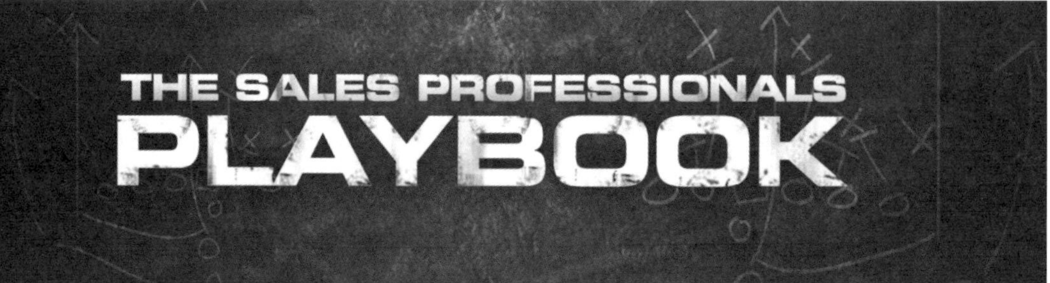




*Quarterly:*

1: ______________________________ 8: ______________________________
2: ______________________________ 9: ______________________________
3: ______________________________ 10: ______________________________
4: ______________________________ 11: ______________________________
5: ______________________________ 12: ______________________________
6: ______________________________ 13: ______________________________
7: ______________________________ 14: ______________________________

**Important Note:** It is recommended that family names not be listed in your prospect lists.

**Networking**

What kind of networking groups are you a part of now?

______________________________________________________________________

______________________________________________________________________

What are some networking groups you would like to pursue but haven't taken the time (by the way, take the time if they are worth it), and what do you hope to gain?

______________________________________________________________________

______________________________________________________________________

______________________________________________________________________

______________________________________________________________________

______________________________________________________________________

______________________________________________________________________

______________________________________________________________________

______________________________________________________________________

List the "follow your dollar" locations that you could put in your sphere:

______________________________________________________________________

______________________________________________________________________

______________________________________________________________________

______________________________________________________________________

**Working the sphere**

Sales professionals need to invest in a relationship before a client will invest in them. Think of your last big sale (older than 30 days). Have you contacted this customer in the last month? ________________ If not, why not? _____________________________

What is a small nugget of information you could send your sphere about your business that you could then follow up with them about? This "nugget" needs to be something informative, interesting and relevant to them:

_______________________________________________________________________

_______________________________________________________________________

_______________________________________________________________________

_______________________________________________________________________

_______________________________________________________________________

*The formula for success (you can tweak one that works for you)*

You need at least three times the number of people in your sphere to make or exceed quota. For example: Monthly goal: $100,000. Average sale per client: $10,000. Number of needed prospects in monthly sphere: 33-34

What is your monthly goal for sales? ____________
What is your average sale per client? ____________
Number of needed prospects in your monthly sphere: ____________

Those in your quarterly are gravy, but they are necessary as they fall into a schedule that affects your monthly output.

The prospect pipeline is like strands on a spider web: the more you have, the sturdier the web; and if one strategy is low, the others keep the web in place.

*Above all, remember to practice!*

**Tele-Prospecting** **Chapter 10**

**pros·pect·ing** (prŏs′ pĕkt′) n. 1. *Pursuing prospects*

Regardless of where your prospects come from—vertical markets, industry contacts, referrals, Google search engines, trade magazines, etc—you still have to *make the calls*. Tele-Prospecting, like all kinds of prospecting, stinks. It is the worst part of any sales job; however, the more sales professionals can do it, the more successful they will be.

The sales professional that prospects religiously will typically be the H __ __ __ __ __ __ one paid.

Rate how much you like prospecting (1 being the lowest, 10 being the highest) ___________

Prospecting is ____% discipline and ____% skill set, but ____% ***necessary***.

**Discipline**

When was the last time you picked up the phone to tele-prospect? __________________

What is the chief benefit of tele-prospecting versus in person prospecting? ____________

What are other benefits of tele-prospecting? ____________________________________

*Make the time*

Because tele-prospecting is usually the least liked thing to do, when is the best time to do it? ______________.

Schedule tele-prospecting (like all prospecting) like an A __ __ __ __ __ __ __ __ __ __.

Don't stop tele-prospecting just because you've reached a P __ __ __.

When in your daily and weekly schedule will you tele-prospect: ____________________

*Stick to it!*

**Skill Set**

Prospects don't like rejecting sales professionals anymore than sales professionals like being rejected.

In order to move a prospect up or out of rotation, use the *3 X 48 program*. Explain what this is: ______________________________________________

***1st call:*** The goal of the 1st call is to introduce yourself to the prospective customer and ask him or her to call you back. Write out your example:

______________________________________________
______________________________________________
______________________________________________
______________________________________________
______________________________________________

***2nd call:*** The goal of the 2nd call is to let the prospect know you are following up to the call you left a couple of days ago (hence 48, as calls should be made every 48 hours apart). Write out your example:

______________________________________________
______________________________________________
______________________________________________
______________________________________________
______________________________________________

**3rd call:** The goal of the 3rd call is 1) to let the prospects know you are not trying to pester them and 2) to give them permission to reject you (this call is key). Write out your example:

______________________________________________
______________________________________________
______________________________________________
______________________________________________
______________________________________________

Why should the 3 X 48 program be successful?

________________________________________________________

________________________________________________________

________________________________________________________

What are some obstacles that you have faced when tele-prospecting?

________________________________________________________

________________________________________________________

________________________________________________________

How can you eliminate these obstacles?

________________________________________________________

________________________________________________________

________________________________________________________

*Scrimmaging tele-prospecting is key!* Who can you scrimmage tele-prospecting with?

________________________________________________________

________________________________________________________

When (like, when in the next 48 hours): ________________________________

*Above all, remember to practice!*

**The Golden T** **Chapter 11**

gold·en (gōl´dən) adj. 1. *Having a promising future; seemingly assured of success*

You have the ability to turn every one of your appointments into three more new opportunities. One of the biggest mistakes sales professionals make is going to their appointments and then leaving to go back to the office or just go on to their next appointment.

A strategic method of door-to-door sales: *visit three businesses that neighbor the one you have an appointment with.*

**Discipline**

Where is your next in person appointment? ______________________________
When? ______________
Whom are you meeting? ________________________

Thinking of this appointment: what businesses can you visit? (*If you don't know, look them up!*)

1:____________________________________________________________
2:____________________________________________________________
3:____________________________________________________________

Being YOU, what can you say to introduce yourself to these Golden T prospects?

____________________________________________________________
____________________________________________________________
____________________________________________________________
____________________________________________________________
____________________________________________________________
____________________________________________________________
____________________________________________________________
____________________________________________________________

*A Golden Demeanor*

A great feature of The Golden T is it is T ___ ___ ___ E ___ ___ ___ ___ ___ ___ ___ ___. You are already there; all you have to do is walk in the door.

Do not L ___ ___. Be honest; be YOU. Think about a time when you were approached by a gimmicky sales person: how did you feel about that person?

_______________________________________________

_______________________________________________

Remember that you are transferring energy during these prospect visits; transfer P ___ ___ ___ ___ ___ ___ ___ energy.

What is the hardest part of doing The Golden T?

_______________________________________________

_______________________________________________

If you don't do much in person prospecting (national phone tele-marketer), what are some ways to use The Golden T program, but via the phone:

_______________________________________________

_______________________________________________

*Do the math*

How many appointments per week is your goal to complete? ____________________

If you Golden T each of these appointments, how many more will you complete?

____________________

Assuming a 50% close ratio, how many MORE closes a week will The Golden T help you achieve? ____________________

*Above all, remember to practice!*

ap·point·ment (ə-point′mənt) n. 1. *An arrangement to do something or meet someone at a particular time and place*

Before going on a sales call, it is important that a sales professional is prepared. I mean *fully* prepared, like a football player would prepare for a game. A sales professional needs to have company information about whoever they are meeting, an agenda, a list of purposeful questions, and must absolutely scrimmage the call with a coach or team member prior to the appointment.

*What about the info?*

What are some ways that you research a company's information in order to be prepared for an appointment? (***Caution:*** *don't go to your appointment and start reciting the history of the company!*)

1: ______________________________

2: ______________________________

3: ______________________________

4: ______________________________

5: ______________________________

**Having an agenda**

It is crucial to have an agenda AT your appointment (hint: bring it with you). No amount of memorization can replace having a *real* agenda with you.

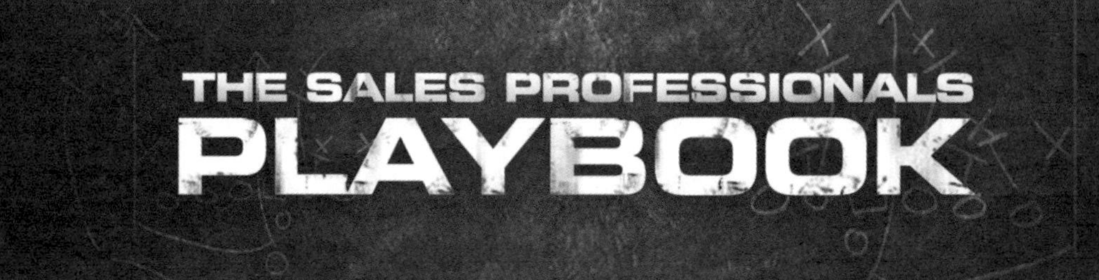




What should your agenda look like for you?

- ________________________________________
- ________________________________________
- ________________________________________
- ________________________________________
- ________________________________________
- ________________________________________
- ________________________________________

*Preparation*

Remember when you developed your purposeful questions?

Now is the time to P __ __ __ __ them and take them with you.

If you do nothing else, scrimmage your appointment before you go. Name at least three people you can scrimmage an appointment with (*Remember, no role-playing—scrimmage!*):

1: ____________________
2: ____________________
3: ____________________

Prepare your prospect; explain your agenda. When you run into a situation where a prospect just wants the basics, what can you respond with?

________________________________________________
________________________________________________
________________________________________________
________________________________________________

Be open about the T __ __ __ you need to do your J __ __.

**Setting the thermostat**

How would your current customers describe your thermostat or energy?

____________________________________________________________

____________________________________________________________

**Elevator speech**

What is your "elevator speech"? Remember it needs to be less than 30 seconds.

____________________________________________________________

____________________________________________________________

____________________________________________________________

____________________________________________________________

**Closing the next step**

Every appointment should have a close. A real close ensures there is a next step-even if that next step is a follow up *scheduled* appointment.

Circle items below that qualify as closes (*Hint: two of them are not closes*):

- No thank you
- Contract signed
- An agreement to follow up in the future
- A meeting for the following Tuesday to finalize details
- An enthusiasm for the product and the prospect wanting to learn more at a later time

*At this point, you have earned the right to ask for the sale; do not leave without exercising that right.*

**Review**

**Circle TRUE (T) or FALSE (F) for each of the following statements.**

T / F 1. Professional sales requires taking to heart vague expressions about sales.

T / F 2. Professional sales requires constant practice.

T / F 3. Treat prospective customers as if they are your uptight neighbor.

T / F 4. Establish likability, trust and influence with your prospective customer!

T / F 5. If a prospect trusts you, it doesn't matter if he or she likes you.

T / F 6. Never bring up your product's disadvantages.

T / F 7. If a prospect raises objections, excuse yourself for a quick bathroom break.

T / F 8. The answers you receive to your purposeful questions should mark the main points on your map of solutions.

T / F 9. Instead of *overcoming* objections, sales professionals should help the prospect *consider all options*.

T / F 10. Keep your sales plan a secret. In a locked safe is best.

T / F 11. You don't need permission to keep calling a prospect. Just do it.

T / F 12. The 3 x 48 program involves making three calls over 48 days.

T / F 13. Return to the office immediately after each sales call to check messages.

T / F 14. Schedule scrimmages whenever you can, but don't sweat cancelling them.

T / F 15. The elevator speech is what you'd say if trapped in an elevator for hours.

T / F 16. Let the prospect ask for the sale.

T / F 17. Make the sale, even if the product is a poor fit for the prospect.